A
BROKEN
Wing

A BROKEN Wing

Dr. Linda N. Cameron

Ordering Information:

For orders and inquiries, please contact:
1-888-404-1388
www.goldtouchpress.com
book.orders@goldtouchpress.com

Printed in the United States of America

"A broken wing is a hurtful thing," was a bird's weak and sad mutter whose wing would not sweep, bend, or flutter.

"It's impossible to fly however hard you try

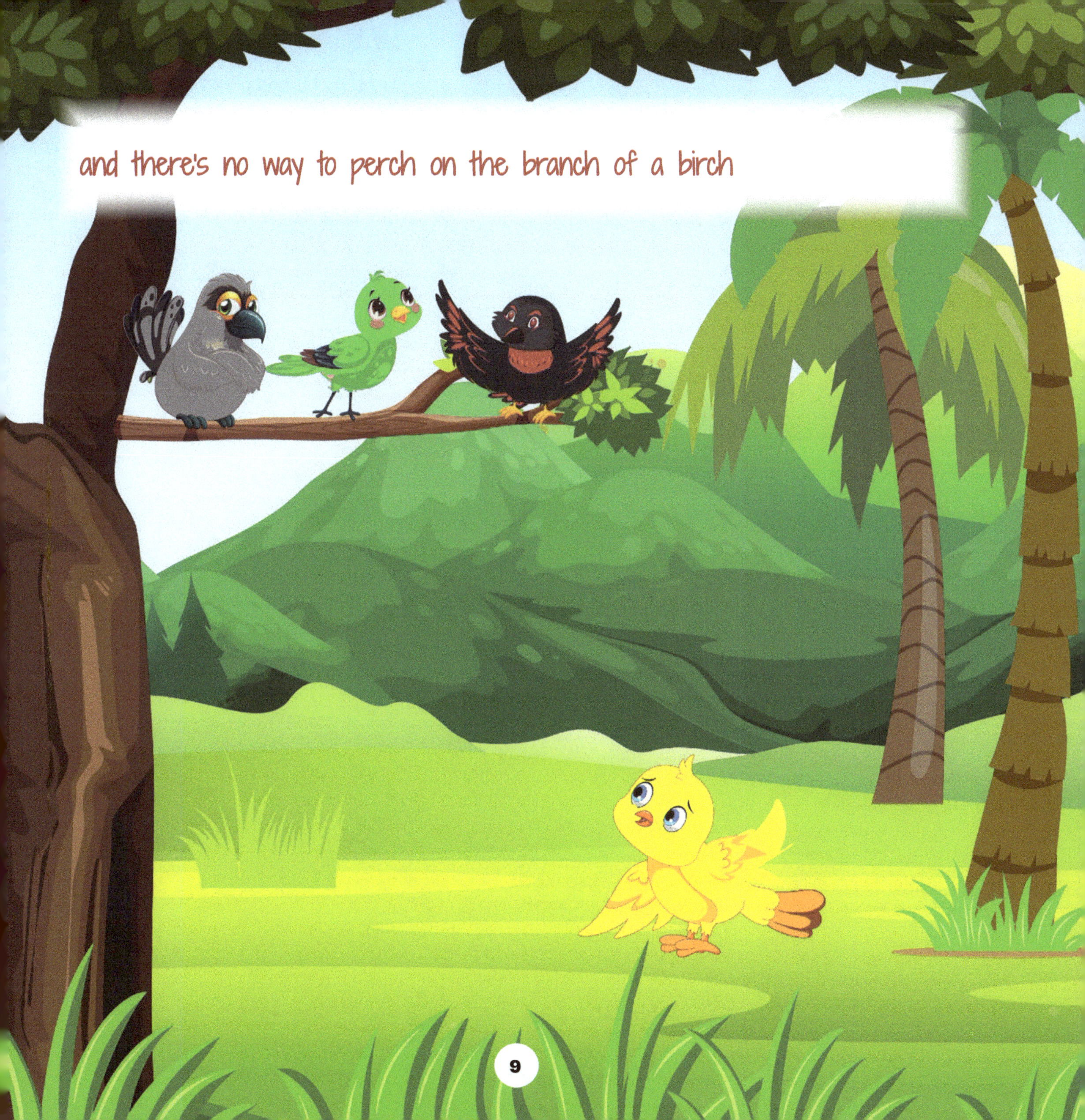
and there's no way to perch on the branch of a birch

or munch on a bunch of ants for your lunch.

"A broken wing is such a hurtful thing, I'll never sing again!" and the bird began to cry.

"But a grasshopper leaping nearby heard his loud, weeping cry and said "Come hop with me and don't try to fly. "Hopping is too slow and not a way for birds to go," came the proud word from the small bird. And he began to cry again.

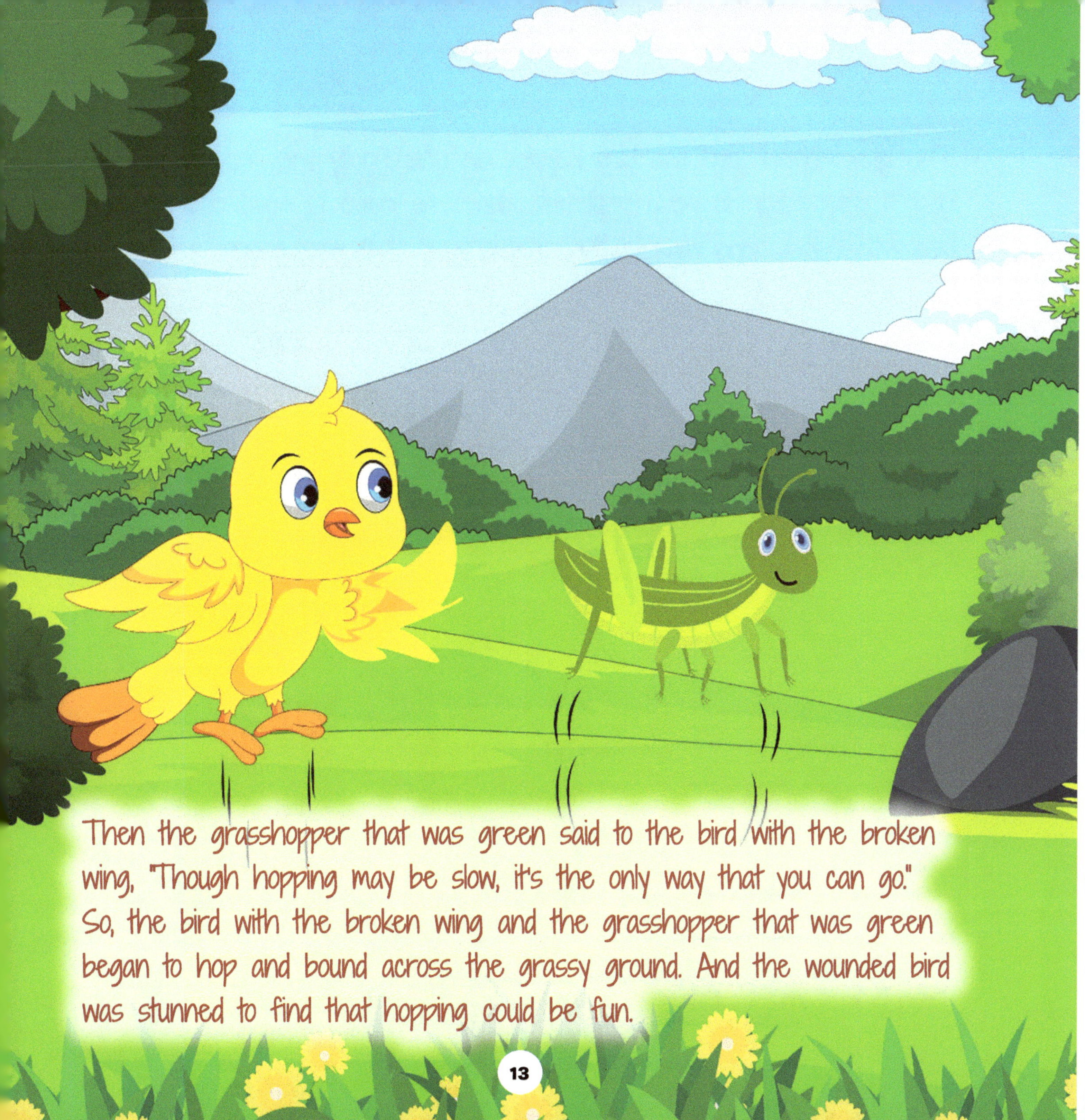

Then the grasshopper that was green said to the bird with the broken wing, "Though hopping may be slow, it's the only way that you can go." So, the bird with the broken wing and the grasshopper that was green began to hop and bound across the grassy ground. And the wounded bird was stunned to find that hopping could be fun.

The grasshopper and the bird hopped on until finally they had to take a rest. "I don't mean to be a pest but I have no place to nest," churred the bird with the broken wing to the grasshopper that was green.

"I can't sleep down on the ground for hungry creatures may come around and eat me feathers, bones, and beak." The grasshopper shuddered to hear him speak and the bird began to cry and tears flowed down around his small beak.

A dragonfly nearby heard the bird's sad cry and asked the grasshopper that was green why the bird was crying.

"He has a broken wing you see and he can't perch in a tree," was the bird's reply to the dragonfly.

"Come follow me!" beckoned the dragonfly, "I'll show you a place to perch that's higher than the branch of a tree!"

So, all three set out on their journey. The bird with a broken wing and the grasshopper that was green began their hops again while the dragonfly that was slim darted around in front of them.

Upon reaching her place the dragonfly darted over and said in a loud cry, "Look up into the sky." The bird looked up and what he saw filled his heart with joy and awe. There rose a cliff of mighty rocks far above the tall treetops. Without another word they headed up the cliff. The dragonfly flew while the grasshopper hopped and the bird did too. At the top of the cliff, they looked around at the sky and the sea and the ground. "Aren't we high?", cried the dragonfly, "Don't you agree, it's better than a tree?" "What a beautiful scene," replied the grasshopper that was green.

But the bird with the broken wing was unable to speak for he had a wiggling thing in his beak. "My friend that's not a worm," said that dragonfly with concern. "Yes, if you don't mind, silly bird," snapped the lanky lizard, "This tail does belong to me." "I'm sorry, I'm sorry," chirped the bird, "But I'm so hungry I thought your tail was a wiggling worm all long and pale!" And the bird began to cry again.

After a quick check of her tail, the lizard cocked her head and said, "It seems to be quite well." "Now if you're hungry come with me." said the lizard to all three. "I'll show you a place full of juicy seeds that will more than meet your needs.

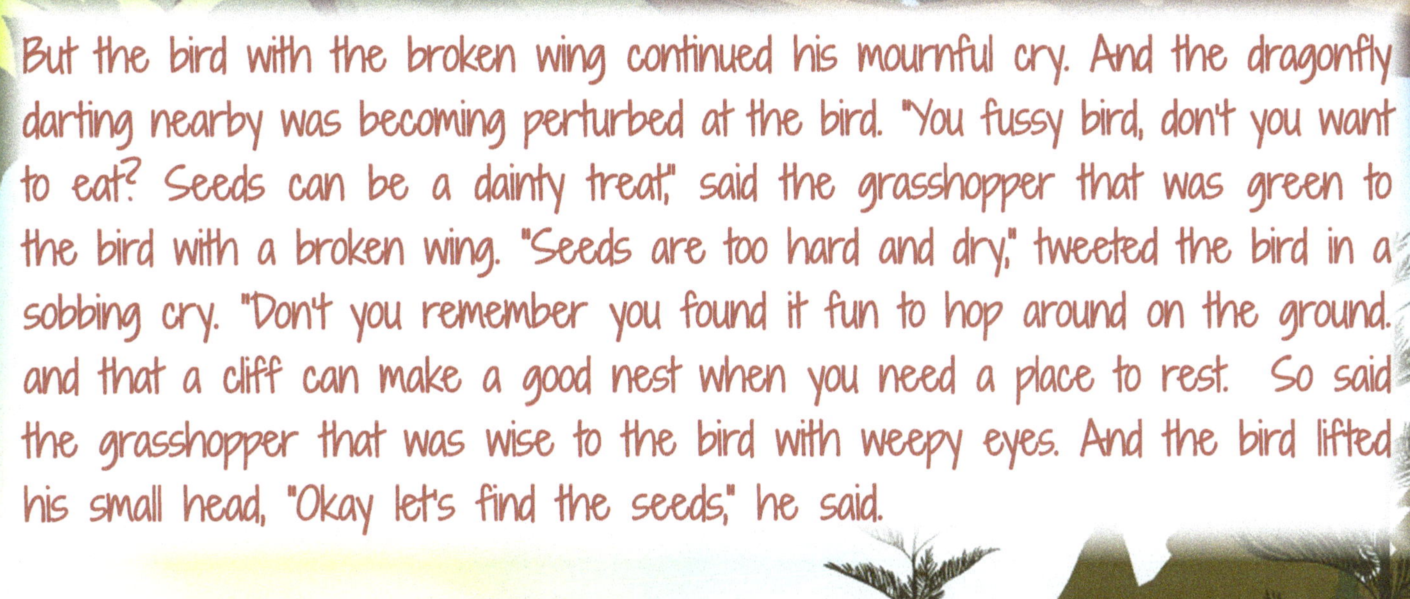

But the bird with the broken wing continued his mournful cry. And the dragonfly darting nearby was becoming perturbed at the bird. "You fussy bird, don't you want to eat? Seeds can be a dainty treat," said the grasshopper that was green to the bird with a broken wing. "Seeds are too hard and dry," tweeted the bird in a sobbing cry. "Don't you remember you found it fun to hop around on the ground. and that a cliff can make a good nest when you need a place to rest. So said the grasshopper that was wise to the bird with weepy eyes. And the bird lifted his small head, "Okay let's find the seeds," he said.

So the bird with a broken wing and the grasshopper that was green hopped behind the lanky lizard as she shimmied down to the ground while the dragonfly that was slim darted around on either side of them.

When they arrived at the lizard's place, the bird began to eat with haste. He picked and pecked without delay for all the rest of this summer day. When his gizzard filled up to the top he returned with his friends to the cliff of rocks.

And though his wing was still stiff and sore, the bird began to sing once more. And this is the song that he sang with a roar. "A broken wing is not such an awful thing. Before I knew only how to fly, but now I can hop right by. Before I knew only how to nest in a tree, but now I can rest on a cliff, you see. Before I liked only ants on trees, but now I can eat juicy seeds. "So a broken wing is not such a hurtful thing!"

And then one day while trying to jerk a worm from the ground the bird's wing began to work. At first his wing began to flicker and flutter and finally it swooped up and down taking him away from the ground.

And the bird flew away that very day.